Discover your

A BEGINNER'S
GUIDE
TO THE
Soul

Jennifer ♥ Lyall

Ebook ISBN: 978-1-7773029-1-7

First printing, 2020 ISBN: 978-1-7773029-0-0

Jennifer Lyall

www.jlyall.com

TABLE OF CONTENTS

FOREWORD

A Beginners Guide to the Soul is your opportunity to learn how to connect with your soul and tap into your inner knowing of how to live a fulfilled life full of love, joy, happiness and playfulness.

Together, we will delve deeply into different areas of your soul. You can think of this book as a sort of owner's manual – the one you wish you came with when you were born; the one you wish you knew how to read when you were born. Actually, I will even say that it's the owner's manual you knew innately when you were born but simply forgot about and lost touch with as you became accustomed with the outer world.

When a baby is born, it is so beautiful and pure – a gift from heaven, so to speak – just as you are today. The difference between a newborn baby and who you are today is that you've had disappointments, celebrations, challenges, breakdowns, and breakthroughs along the way that have caused you to remember and forget who you truly are.

Throughout life, we are taught routines to keep our body healthy. From a young age, we are encouraged to brush our teeth at least twice a day, to eat breakfast as good fuel for our body and to have a bath or shower regularly. These are wonderful practices for our physical body; the emotional, spiritual, and intellectual aspects of ourselves need the same level of regular nurturing. This guide will review what this means, and the many ways you can feed your soul.

Each chapter contains "Soul Joy." These are exercises to open up and deepen your connection with your soul. The exercises are easy, short and intended to nurture the inner dialogue with your soul.

iv

The intention of A Beginners Guide to the Soul is to gently show you how to return to the purity, innocence and playfulness that you innately are. Your life is meant to be full of joy and bliss in anything and everything that you do. My heart's desire is to provide you with a new perspective to consider that will help you get back to that state of being.

I honour the light in you. Namaste~

Jennifer Lyall

CHAPTER 1: WHO AM I?

Who am I?

This is such a simple question and yet such a profound inquiry at the same time. When we are challenged or confronted by life's difficulties – or when we are sitting in peaceful contemplation – we ponder, "Who Am I?"

To be quite honest, a better question to begin with would be, "Who am I *not*?"

Who you are not is all of those things that you think you are. That may seem a little strange, but let me express it in another context. People often live their life with judgments of the experiences they have. These judgments may be their own, or from others. Over time, these judgments pile up, and people form a perception of who they are; but the judgments are merely the labels they have given themselves based on the experiences they have had. These labels are not who they are.

"Who am I?" is actually a very beautiful question. Who you are is love. The very core of you is love. This may be difficult to consider for someone who has seemingly had an unloving life. This may be hard for someone to accept if they feel they are unlovable. This may be challenging for someone to comprehend, based on what their perceptions of love are.

I'm not talking about idealized, romantic love; I'm referring to something much more profound and deeper than that...and yet simpler. It is that beautiful feeling in your heart when you watch the rain fall, or when you stop and smell the sweet roses. It is that warm feeling in your heart when you pause and look at a magical rainbow, or when you take a moment to watch a baby's precious smile. It is that feeling of amazement when you see an incredible nature photo of an animal captured in the moment of simply being who they are. That's love.

The feelings of peace, joy, love are all intermingled. It's that warm feeling in your heart that's actually pumping and radiating out who you are: you are love.

Now, somebody who may have been surrounded by misfortunes or perceived mis-fortunes may have a hard time grasping this concept; but I guarantee that if you search your heart you will recognize this feeling quite easily, as it comes naturally to human beings.

The thing to always remember is that an experience is not who you are. If you didn't sing your best at a talent show, or you weren't selected for a school play, you simply did not succeed in that event. You did not meet the expectations of the people who were deciding who or what they were looking for in that instance. That does not make you a failure, a bad singer or untalented. It doesn't make you any less of a person. It was simply an experience.

This chapter is really about the distinction between who you are as a human being (who we *all* really are as human beings) versus the labels we put on ourselves in our experiences. They are two very different things.

Sometimes I feel that life is like a video game. There are various strategies you can take to make sure your character makes it through one level after another. These strategies could include monitoring your health, hiding or moving in a manner to stay safe; and clobbering or evading the bad guys. Moving through different levels in a video game is like going through different stages of life, with the challenges getting a little more demanding as you progress. All games must end, and when it's over…well, at least you feel good knowing you played your best, right?

When you can observe your life from the perspective of a gamer (someone who plays lots of video games), you can see that every experience is simply a moment. The accumulation of moments bundle together to form events. The sequence of events creates the game, or the life. The experiences are not "real;" it is just something that has happened. What "appears real" is your perception of what that experience "means." The experiences do not affect who that character is, fundamentally.

For instance: say you choose character A in a game, and as you play you have an experience that makes you smaller temporarily. The innate qualities of character A have not changed; their abilities have just been adjusted for a short period of time. If during that period you encounter a "bad guy" and take a pounding, then your perception of Character A may have change; yet Character A has not really changed. She still moves in the same way, operates in the same way; she merely performs differently for a moment, then gets back to her old self.

To look at life from the observer's perspective – as if you are witness to life – can be freeing.

It's called living detached from the outcomes; it is about letting go of judgment and worry to live full out, in a loving and honourable manner.

You may not be able to live like this 100% of the time. For me, it took time to understand how to not get tangled up in other people's energy all of the time. It took time to let go of emotions, let go of needing to control things, needing to know the answers. I still notice I get caught up in needing to know things, but I don't get as worked up about it as I used to.

I found that meditation helped me tremendously with learning how to let go of thoughts, ideas and emotions. I have done a lot of energy clearing with other practitioners, but mostly with myself over the years. It has helped me to understand some of the physical and emotional feelings that come up inside of me, and let them go.

Journaling also helped me with this. When I can let ideas, thoughts, and emotions out on paper, then put the journal aside and come back to it later, I can look at things from a new perspective and witness how I was feeling.

I have become familiar with a technique called "mirroring" that I have actively done with friends, and also with clients, to support them. Mirroring is when someone says something, and the other person listening reflects or repeats back what they heard, including the tone of voice, body language, and emotion that the person speaking is projecting that they may not be aware of. My kids also do a good job of reflecting things back to me, so if I'm not aware of the impact of what I'm saying, they will let me know. It causes me to pause and consider: is that the message I really want to be sending, or can I share it another way?

All of these tools have helped me to learn how to become more detached from situations and understand if there is something in that situation that is bothering me, or if it is stirring up emotions from the past. If there is, I then check-in with myself as to what are the best next steps.

What is an Experience?

An experience is what you hear, think, see, taste or feel, in a moment or in a series of moments. Every person in the world has a different life experience.

Imagine 10 people standing around a beautiful garden. Each person will have a different experience, based on their perspective around this garden; this is true for everything in life. While someone may be caught up in the awe and beauty of a flower that has just opened, they may not see the butterfly fluttering on the other side of the bush.

4

The butterfly may not be within view, or they may be so intent on observing the flower – or even focused on it being too hot outside – that they miss the butterfly floating by.

It doesn't make their experience any better or worse than the person who observes the butterfly, it is just *different*. It doesn't make that person a better person for observing the opening of the flower. It doesn't make them less of a person for being too hot. It is just *different,* and beautiful for being present with that opportunity. To be. To live. To learn.

Now imagine a picture of two people. The person on the right is the pure embodiment of love; they have let go of labels.

Labelled **Has Let Go of Labels**

The person on left wears several labels, based on experiences throughout their life.

Perhaps when they were young they fought with their older brother. They were much smaller and gained the label of a *wimp*. Maybe that family had a lot of money, and yet was so empty. They always bought and bought and bought, yet they were never fulfilled with what they thought they wanted. So maybe *unsatisfied* is the label that person would add. Perhaps they failed second grade and then they labeled themselves a *failure*. It hung over them through their entire educational career. It could be that in high school that they told someone they liked them, but were rejected, and labeled themselves as unlovable.

Using the image provided here, I want you to take a second look at the person the right. Their experiences have been simply accepted as moments in life and have rolled off them; much like water rolling off a duck's back. That individual has not carried the weight of those experiences as thoughts and labels through their life. They are able to move forward as love.

Who would you rather be – the person free of the labels, or the person with the labels?

Story: Unrewarding Career - Lost who I am

I was speaking with a friend of mine – "Susan" – about soul searching, and asking the question **Who Am I?** She shared how over the years of being married, becoming a mother, having crazy family dynamics, and being in a job that is unrewarding, that she feels like she has lost a little bit of who she is.

What I discovered, for me, is that as I tried to control all the areas of my life by adapting who I was being or trying to dominate others, I changed. I let their labels of me – and ironically, my labeling of them – affect who I was being in the world. While I was trying to influence and change others (I'll be honest here, sometimes it was even bullying), my actions actually took the biggest toll on myself and my connection to my soul.

To put it another way: me living up to their labels and molding myself based on who I perceived them to be took me further away from my True Self. And on top of it, I was being mean because I thought my way was the right way, so I was trying to convince them to come around to my point of view. Talk about draining!

Good News!

I have good news: these labels come off quite easily, because in every single moment you can recreate yourself. I had to do this in order to move forward in my life. Things just weren't working with me trying to fit into this other "mold."

Now, you may think, "there's no way I can ever do that. My whole family has labeled me that way." I invite you to consider that you can declare who you are in any given moment. You can decide who you are going to be at any time; you can choose to continue to live your life as those labels, or start to let go of the labels and show people who you truly are.

Apply the same concept to two dolls that are for sale. One doll doesn't have a box; it is just on the shelf, made lovingly with care. The other doll is in a box, with all of these labels on it. I'm sure you've seen those products with a long list of claims about what it is or does, plastered all over the box. Do you want to live your life constrained by a box and the labels? Or, do you want to live your life freely as the toy that's made with love? It's your choice. It's your life to live, no one else's.

This brings me back to the question: *Who am I?*

You are the only person who can answer that question. You can talk to friends to see what their perception is of you. It may give you some insight into some strengths you didn't realize you have. Ultimately, only you can answer the question "Who am I?"

Who Am I? is an important question for anyone and everyone to consider. Ask yourself right now, in this moment: Who Am I? Draw a picture of yourself; it can be a stick person like the one in the diagram. Then write all of the words describing who you are that come into your heart.

I can guarantee you that if you can do this and let your *heart* speak the words, that each word will be an expression of love. Therefore, if you are a graceful dancer and you write *I am a graceful dancer,* that is an expression of love. If you are a talented builder, that is an expression of love. If you are a creative writer, that is an expression of love. If you are an amazing singer, that is an expression of love. If you are a master gardener, that is an expression of love. All of those things are about creation. Creation is the ultimate expression of love. Anything that you create from your heart is an expression of love.

Even if you sing a song that is someone else's words, you add your own flair to it, creating variations in the tones that only you can sing; that's your expression of love. Anything that you create with your mind, your voice, your words, and your hands represent expressions of love, regardless of who developed the "original" version.

Do you get that? You are a master creator expressing love in everything that you do. You express yourself in what you say, what you write, what you wear, and what you make. All of those expressions share a different side of you.

Soul Joy

Set aside some time to sit down and reflect on "Who am I?" If it helps, draw a stick figure and write your notes next to it.

Let the answers flow from your heart.

If you are not connecting with this concept of you being love, you can come back to this exercise later in the book.

_____

_____

_____

_____

_____

_____

_____

_____

_____

_____

_____

_____

_____

_____

_____

_____

_____

CHAPTER 2: WHAT IS A SOUL?

As with most things in life, there are many interpretations of what a soul is. You can examine the definition of a soul based on scientific research, from the perspective of a philosopher like Plato or Socrates, or you could consider how it is defined by one of the many religions in this world. In the end, you get to decide what a soul is for you, your truth, and your perception of life.

The definition that this book is based upon is my truth of what a soul is.

A soul is a very special part of each person and every being. It is that special essence inside that is eternal and all-knowing; the part of you that always is, always was, and always will be.

I believe everything has a soul. A person, a plant, a desk. I even remember when I was a child; I would say something to the toaster to let it know I still cared for it, even though we were only using the kettle that morning. I wanted it to know that it was still valued. I loved all of my stuffed animals, and in my heart, they were alive. Perhaps my perspective as a child was more right than that which surfaced as I became an adult.

A soul is all-knowing. The soul is like an embodiment of "why" that being or object is in existence; its meaning, or purpose. It's that part of you that really wants to be present fully in the world and has no fear. Your soul knows your true potential. It can do everything and loves everything.

It is that little voice that reminds you of how incredible you are.

It is always present, patiently waiting to reveal itself to you. It's one of the most magnificent elements of a human's existence, and yet it's just starting to be talked about openly. I believe that until we connect with our soul, we cannot tap into our full potential.

If you believe in reincarnation, as I do, you likely share my perception that the soul is the part of you that continues on, lifetime after lifetime after lifetime.

What is life like for a person who lives from the soul?

Fearless

Moving forward

All knowing

Lives their truth

Playful

Practical

Non-judgmental

Welcoming

Peaceful

If we all have souls, then why isn't the whole world peaceful and loving?

I believe that although we have a soul, we become conditioned to our living environment and *forget* that we have one. We become disconnected and go through ups and downs, and thus move through moments of life where we are connected, and other periods where we are not.

It's all perfect, the whole journey of ups and downs; it's just part of the human experience. The contrasts of emotions help us to expand and gain clarity about who we are and what we really want in the world. Just think: if you were to eat your favourite meal every day, you would become bored with it. Eating a variety of food, like experiencing a range of emotions, helps you to better understand and appreciate the subtleties and nuances between the different flavours and feelings.

You can think of a soul being inside of a body as being much like a human trying to operate a giant robot from a seat inside that robot. Imagine being inside of this robot and wanting to go somewhere. You would clumsily step with your feet, hoping to place them down properly and in the right direction.

Much like you being inside of the robot, the soul knows what to do and what this body is capable of, but it has to get through all of these layers of the ego, fear and crazy self-talk in our heads. It has to work through all of this in order to get its message through to you for how to move forward. When there is a lot of static on the communication line, like negative self-talk, other people's opinions, and advertising, the voice of the soul can get lost.

When you are more connected, you get these little signals from your soul – like a gut feeling or goosebumps (or what I like to call *truth bumps*) – when somebody says something that is true. Sometimes it shows up as a voice in your head, or a knowing of what's to come or what to do. When you relinquish control in your life, it's the part of you that takes over. Often times, when we let go of trying to control everything and let the soul work its magic, beauty comes into our lives.

That's what the soul is: the most beautiful part of our being. It's all we are. It's an infinite supply of love and knowing that we can tap into at any moment; we just often forget to connect.

There are so many different ways for people to be more in tune with their soul. The reason for this book is to bring that possibility into your awareness and to know that it can be so simple.

Soul Joy:

Take time to review your personal definition of a soul.

Consider moments when you feel happiest and most connected with your soul. What are you doing? Who are you with?

_____

_____

_____

_____

_____

_____

_____

_____

_____

_____

_____

_____

_____

_____

_____

_____

_____

_____

_____

CHAPTER 3: GOD IS LOVE-*LY*

I believe there is only one creator, known by many names, including Divine, Tao, the One, Source, Allah, creator or God. By whichever name you call this higher power, it is just love-ly. They are love and they are love-ly.

Do you feel the difference between those two words?

They are the same, but slightly different. Love is pure bliss. Love-ly adds delight to the mix; it is the essence of love. It's like comparing a scoop of vanilla ice cream to a scoop of vanilla ice cream served in a pretty bowl with a cherry on top. Do you feel the distinction?

As people discover their connection with God, Source, their soul, the One, they become very aware of this love-ly connection and how much it surrounds them. It fills their heart with delight and with joy. It takes them back to who they truly are. (For now, I'm going to refer to this creator or being as God, and feel free to interchange it with whatever name you like to use.)

As people are on their journeys and discovering who this creator is, some develop beliefs around there being lessons to be learned from their creator. I remember having a conversation with someone and commenting on an experience I had, "I guess it was just a lesson I had to learn." She replied that God doesn't harshly teach us lessons, there are indeed things to learn in life, but they are from a loving place and are part of our evolution.

It is no different from how a child explores the world when the parent will let the child have an experience so they can learn. Sometimes a child may reach out and touch a hot stove or hot kettle. It's a painful moment and a parent can't always be there to stop the child from getting hurt. It's not something that is done out of cruelty; it is simply something that is part of that child's development.

Every lesson and every experience that you are faced with is part of your spiritual development, and that's all there is. You are constantly evolving. My hope for you is that you evolve with ease and grace. Sure, life is going to present challenges, and how you view these situations becomes the same as your perspective or your viewpoint of God.

If you go through a challenging period in your life where everything seems to go wrong at once – say you break a leg and you can't work, and perhaps your spouse loses their job, and your parent's house burns down – you may find yourself in such a low place that you wonder why God is being cruel or unfair. You may even think God is punishing you. Your view of God is reflective of how you are viewing your situation.

The times where you're angry or frustrated are when you forget about your divine connection and your personal divinity. It's okay; it's part of the human experience. There is nothing wrong with having moments when you forget. Those are the times when God will lift you up the most, if you let God.

Those moments when you think you can't go on and can't move forward, and you do – that's when you're tapping into God's love and your soul's wisdom to carry you through.

You are simply being given opportunities to pause, reflect, learn and modify who you are being and what you are doing. It's part of your personal expansion. We're always growing and expanding.

Miracles happen all of the time.

You hear of experiences of "angels" preventing someone from being run over, or saving a person from being hurt. That is God at work; that is Divine intervention.

Now you could be the devil's advocate (so to speak), and ask the questions: Then why are there times when people do get hurt and face immense challenges? Why doesn't God come in at every moment to save everyone?

Challenges bring about opportunities for people to tap into a wonderful strength they didn't know they had. These are opportunities for that person to learn and grow beyond how they are living their life. It's a wake-up call from your soul saying, "You are better than this, you are so much more than this, let's take life to the next level."

Sophie's Story

A few years ago, a friend of mine named Sophie had an incredible experience. She had two young toddlers and worked part-time. Her self-employed husband came home one day and told her that they lost $250,000 in the stock market and that his business was going under. He didn't know how they were going to make their next mortgage payment. Family health issues also came up, as her mother was diagnosed with a rare form of cancer.

Sophie took in all of this information and reflected on the situation. This was her opportunity to learn and grow. She resolved to turn things around for their family and to be strong to support her mother. She got her Real Estate license and committed to doing anything and everything to be successful. She went from selling three houses a year to selling 33 homes in a year. Sophie lives a balanced life with family, work, vacation and self-care, and is in a better place than she would have been if she had not faced that challenge.

Every perceived challenge in life is an opportunity to go beyond how you are currently living and viewing life. It is an invitation to go deeper, be stronger, and live a more fulfilled life.

It is just like a child given a tough assignment at school. Some people swim through the assignment and they are easily able to tackle the project while other people have a harder time. When they persevere, that is when they succeed and make it out on top. They excel when they find the inner strength that is always within them. God's wish is for you to tap into that inner strength, inner peace, and inner knowing. That is my perception of God's will and wish for you.

God knows your true potential. Life presents you with different opportunities to step into that potential. They always hold the space for you to realize the full beauty of you, the reflection of love in this world. I don't quite know how to put words to this. It is simply something I have come to experience, in magical *aha* moments when reading a book, or having a conversation about God or the soul, or through embracing spirituality. It's a feeling I get when I'm fully present (i.e. my mind isn't focused on something else), in nature, or when things fall into place as they do. You can't always see the beautiful weaving of the tapestry when you are so close. It's when you take a step back that you get a full understanding of how everything comes together. It's that feeling – a knowing of being surrounded by a love that believes in me fully.

You, God, and every creation around you is the essence of love. The world is your playground, with limitless possibilities to explore. You and every person around you have the ability to experience whatever your heart desires. With firm intention, action, belief and passion you can see anything through; God and the Universe will be there to support you in incredible ways. Every creation, every soul, is a different expression of perfection, reminding you that beauty and grace comes in many forms.

Look for the beauty and grace in everything and every situation - it is there! You may see it as:

The joyful smile of a young child.

The reflection of the sky on a puddle.

The sound of a joyous melody.

A perfectly ripe peach.

Events magically falling into place to help you achieve your desired result.

The grace of how someone holds the door open for you.

A bird swiftly soaring and maneuvering between trees.

A dancer stepping and spinning across a stage.

The trees swaying in the wind.

God sees the beauty in everything and everyone. He honours that grace and invites you to do the same, appreciating the miracles that surround you. Honouring these miracles for their unique qualities and God-like essence is your opportunity to experience heaven on earth.

Now you need to check in to your heart to see if you feel that as well.

God is love. God is love-ly.

Soul Joy

Reflect on what your divine connection is. What does it feel like and how does it appear in your life?

Take a moment to be present with and notice beauty and grace that you see today. Write down all of these magic moments and take note of how you feel.

_____

_____

_____

_____

_____

_____

_____

_____

_____

_____

_____

_____

_____

_____

_____

_____

_____

_____

_____

_____

_____

_____

_____

_____

_____

_____

_____

_____

_____

_____

CHAPTER 4: WHAT IS LOVE?

Alright, so you feel love in your heart, and you acknowledge and accept the possibility that you are indeed the embodiment of love. But what exactly is love?

Love is an emotion, a feeling, a state of being, and a gift to share. Love is the combination of many different things: joy, happiness, harmony, peace, forgiveness, authenticity, presence, trust, and believing.

Love shows up in so many ways. Romance, hugs, volunteering, dancing in the rain. Love is the place of pure peacefulness that resides within. Love is the state of being that you radiate, an electromagnetic pulse you emit. It's more easily experienced than defined.

Maybe you don't feel love all of the time. Perhaps you have moments when you lapse, and feel fear, worry, unease, and distrust. Those feelings are an absence of love – because if you review what love is, then fear, worry, distrust and doubt can't exist. Let me explain.

Imagine that your body is like a radio tower putting out signals based on your emotions. When your body is broadcasting the frequency of love, it isn't able to send out fear and uncertainty at the same time. When you are playing a love song – at that moment, fear and uncertainty do not exist.

Yes, you will experience fear, doubt, uncertainty, distrust, disbelief, worry, angst, anger, and jealously as you move through life, but it will pass. It always does. You always get back to a place of love. You have the amazing ability to recreate yourself at any given moment.

Consider someone in your life who has overcome an addiction to alcohol, drugs or cigarettes – or Joe Vitale, who went from being homeless to becoming a bestselling author, speaker and musician. Each individual has likely experienced times when they have felt beaten down; or even taken on self-defeating labels like failure, unworthy, or unloving. These labels may have come in the form of their own words and thoughts, or from others. These examples of individuals who have overcome difficult times demonstrate how you can move into a new possibility and create a new life for yourself at any time.

Look at Oprah Winfrey; a magnificent soul. So much love and wisdom to share. And she is human. She came from humble beginnings to build a life of great success. She has had ups and downs emotionally, physically, and spiritually. All sorts of things have happened in her life, and yet she is fantastic at picking herself back up again. She remembers that the inspiration that she radiates out to the world is within herself. She draws on that strength to stand up again.

Oprah Winfrey is a wonderful and incredible woman, and she's no different from anyone else. We all have the same capability; we simply have to believe.

So what is love? Love is a combination of emotions that radiate from your heart to give you that feel-good feeling deep inside. You put out into the universe a high vibrational electromagnetic pulse. It makes you smile and giggle. It makes you want to do wonderful things for yourself and others. That's love.

Loving Yourself

Now, let's talk about loving yourself.

As I talk to friends, family members and clients, I see a repeating pattern: many people forget that it's okay to love yourself. Life gets so busy, that they don't even think of making time to love themselves. Or, they think that it's selfish to do so.

It is so important to make time for being love and loving yourself for who you are. You need to remember to love yourself to keep your personal fountain of love flowing.

Think of a mother, who often times puts herself on the bottom of the list of priorities: taking care of the family, perhaps working full time, and having the responsibility of managing the household. She takes care of the kids, supports her husband, buys the groceries, cooks the meals, cleans the home, keeps on top of the school and family commitments, schedules the family's activities, sets aside time for her social engagements, supports the community and maybe even finds time for her own personal development. Sometimes things get to be a little too much and mothers/women (we all), forget that we need to continue to nurture our soul and to honour and love ourselves so we can have the energy to keep giving love to others.

You need to make yourself the priority.

Just like the instructions in the emergency procedures reviewed on an airplane: if you are traveling with someone and the air pressure in the cabin drops, causing the oxygen masks to release from the ceiling, you are advised to put your mask on first before helping others. If you are not strong, and haven't looked after yourself, then the person you are trying to help won't be able to benefit from you at your best.

Taking the time to love yourself, getting the rest you need, eating good foods, and doing things you enjoy, are the most important investments you can make in you.

When you love yourself first, you are taking care of other people.

Do you get that?

Taking care of you helps others, because when you are peaceful, happy, joyful and living your life from your heart, you can help uplift others so they too can be happy, peaceful and joyful. If you are stressed out, tired, and miserable, you are in no shape to help others be the best they can be. You end up spreading more miserable energy in the world when you are stressed out!

For me, it's getting up early in the morning and completing my own magical routine before everyone else gets up. That's how I keep my vibration high and stay happy and healthy so I can best help my family and others.

In my morning routine, I may dance, stretch, meditate, write, read, sing, chant, journal, create, or simply complete something that requires a peaceful heart space for me to best work on that project.

This is my divine time, and I tune in each morning to see what my mind, body and soul need.

When I have filled my own cup of love, I then have the ability to give everyone else the love that is needed. In this space, there's love to family, love to friends, love to the romance of your life, love to animals, and love to everything else too.

This may seem strange, however – when you are able to give love to everyone in your life, anyone you meet, and to everyone and everything out there in the universe, you are investing in your future.

It's like putting money away for your retirement. When you can send love out there to others, you are making deposits in the "bank of love" that you can withdraw from in a time of future need.

This concept of *being* love is a little different than loving someone or something. Being love is to consciously radiate the love that you are out to the world. Sing that song in your heart joyfully and let it be contagious to everything that surrounds you. Whether it's the cat, the kids, the cashier at the store, or the flowers, they all feel your love. Be the love, be the change, be present; it's all the same thing.

How can you *be* love?

Think of your happy place. It could even be a moment when you are sitting in the sun and you feel the sunbeams warming your skin. In that moment, you feel peace, joy and bliss. A smile spreads on your face. Your heart begins to expand. That is being love. Imagine feeling like that all the time - floating gracefully through life. Now, imagine how the people around you feel when you are being like that?

Good moods are contagious!

Soul Joy

Write a love note to yourself, letting yourself know how much you appreciate you.

Think of something you love to do that you haven't done in a long time - go do it! It could be anything, even a hot bath, a pedicure, or reading a book. Make time for things you love this week. And write down how you feel when you do them.

Create an I Love Myself song and sing it at the top of your lungs!

Where is your happy place? Go there physically or in your imagination. Spend some time there then write about how you feel.

CHAPTER 5: HONOUR THYSELF

In today's busy society, we have so much to do that we often put our own health and well-being at the bottom of the list. It is important to recognize that we need to nurture ourselves in order to perform and achieve what we are meant to do in life.

One analogy I love with respect to making time to honour yourself comes from ancient Tao teachings. In Chinese philosophy, the Tao is the underlying universal principal that is signified by yin and yang, or the "code of behaviour" that is in harmony with natural order. One Tao teaching from the Tao Te Ching (which is the interpretation of these principals) talks about how each of us is like an oil lamp. When we are born, our lamp is full of oil. When our oil runs out, the light of the lamp is extinguished, as is our earthly experience; we die. According to the teaching, if you never add oil to your lamp, your lamp will extinguish faster. You replenish the oil in your lamp by taking time to take care of and honour yourself.

We touched on this concept a little bit in the previous chapter when we talked about loving yourself, but I want to delve a little deeper into what it really means to honour yourself.

For me, the distinction between loving yourself and honouring yourself is that loving yourself is the act of what you do to take care of you. Honouring yourself is about appreciating, acknowledging and respecting yourself as a person, and setting boundaries and creating time to love yourself.

To honour yourself is to honour the beauty that is within you and this body that allows you to experience life. To honour yourself is to take the time to recharge your batteries, to put more oil in your lamp.

To recharge yourself is to dedicate yourself to a daily practice. A practice is creating time and space in your day for a routine of activities that nurture your mind, body and soul.

In my upbringing in Canada, I was not introduced to the concept of a practice. At the time, my family did not go to church and we didn't have any special daily routines. My parents had their own business and worked long hours. Life was more about surviving than thriving.

I developed a perception of people in countries like India, China, and Japan taking time for prayer and meditation every day. I would curiously watch television programs and see people praying, or see my co-workers slip out at lunchtime to pray or do special rituals to observe holidays. It seems that as different cultures have settled in North America, and as younger generations became North Americanized, some of these beautiful traditions got forgotten, because they didn't fit this continent's lifestyle.

Thankfully, these concepts are not totally lost. Some continued to honour themselves with a daily practice, whether they retained their culture's traditions, or were worldly travelers and insightful students who learned about these traditions and created a personal practice that they integrate easily into their lives. Thankfully, celebrations of multicultural traditions and multi-faith practices are becoming more common.

A practice becomes a habit, no different from your bedtime routine. When you get ready for bed, you may brush your teeth, wash your face, comb your hair, put your pajamas on and close your eyes. It is the routine you created to do every day to prepare for sleep. Now what if you followed a routine to help ensure you have a good day?

Creating a practice is simply a matter of valuing the experience (of meditation, movement, etc.) and setting aside the time every day to do it. To me, a practice incorporates activities that honour not only your physical body and your mental body, but it also nurtures your soul.

There are many different things that can be included in your practice. Below are a few that you can incorporate into your daily routine. I can guarantee that by creating and being disciplined in your practice, you will notice shifts in your life and your perceptions. Investing time in your practice honours your soul, honours you and gives yourself the time to reflect on "who am I?" while remembering you are love at your very core.

Some of the activities that can be performed within your practice are:

Meditation

Movement

Mindfulness

Writing/journaling

Breathing

Chanting/affirmations

Being in Nature

Expressing Gratitude/Appreciation

Blessing

Prayer

A practice can incorporate any or all of these activities and can include many others, too. They do not need to be experienced at the exact same time each day, although that does facilitate creating a habitual routine, which will ensure greater success to continuing a practice.

You do not need to take on every aspect all at once. You could do some in the morning, several at lunchtime, and others in the evening. Some of these activities you can do throughout your day, like chanting. You need to look at your own lifestyle and determine what suits you and naturally fits in to implement your practice with ease.

As with any new habit that you are forming, be gentle with yourself, and consider keeping track of what you do to celebrate your success and acknowledge what you are accomplishing.

The changes that you will feel in your heart will surprise you as your perceptions soften and your heart opens.

Meditation

Some people have a perception that to meditate you need to sit on a pillow on the floor with your hands in a particular formation, your legs crossed, and chanting *Om~*.

While some people do meditate in this fashion, there are several methods of meditating. Meditation has been a part of different religions and cultures for thousands of years. This exercise is about taking the time to go on a journey within, a journey to connect with your soul and heart; an opportunity to let go of thoughts, and give your mind and body a break. When you have over 60,000 thoughts in a day, it gets a little exhausting for your mind. You can think of meditation as a mini vacation for your mind.

It is also a special time for your soul and your heart. Your heart can sometimes get caught up in the emotional stories in your mind, taking you out of alignment with your soul. When you meditate, those stories disappear for a brief moment, allowing your heart, mind and soul a chance to simply be.

Getting started with meditation may seem like a daunting task. Your mind races, wondering how to cease the stream of thoughts. Your ego nags you, telling you that you don't have the time or patience to meditate.

The truth is, as you get started with meditating, you will still have thoughts. Even yogis who have been meditating for years still have thoughts come into their mind during meditation. The trick is to let the thoughts go as quickly as they come.

Think about sitting down at the doctor's office, flipping through a magazine. You briefly look at the pictures, but continue to flip the pages, not being absorbed or focused on any particular article or advertisement. You see the page; you notice it and flip to the next one. In meditation, when the thought enters the mind, you bring your attention back to your meditation – perhaps to the sound of your breath, or the sound of the voice of the person leading the guided meditation, or the sound of the music in the background – and let the thoughts go.

Sometimes these thoughts may be a running list of the tasks you need to complete that day. As you are able to surrender to the silence and peacefulness, the thought may come in the form of an answer to a question or problem you are having, or an inspiration for something new for you to create.

Those are the fruits of your labour: inner peace, more heart-driven creativity and manifestation, filling your oil lamp, recharging your batteries, healing yourself, and giving your mind, heart, ego and soul a break.

You have access to meditation support right at your fingertips through books, CDs, websites, courses, and even groups – right in your community – that meet to meditate.

There are so many different ways to meditate – you can find a style that helps you ease into a routine. Different approaches to meditating include:

Moving meditations

Guided meditations

Sitting in stillness and silence

Group meditations

Breathing meditations

Visual meditations

Chanting meditations

Look into the different options that suit your lifestyle. There are even meditations geared towards people who find it hard to meditate.

Mediate every day, even if you start with a simple five-minute mediation in silence. It doesn't cost you a penny. You can use tools like a timer to make sure you don't meditate too long, as you get used to your practice. Enjoy it; connect to the feeling, the peace inside, and the insights and little treasures you get in that exercise and throughout your day.

How to incorporate meditation into your practice:

Ideally, begin your day with meditation.

Add it to the middle or end of your day.

Since there are meditations to help you get to sleep, as you get started with meditation, you could do so before bedtime.

Movement

We hear so much about how we need to get our bodies moving so we are healthier. The focus of movement is often on keeping flexible, burning calories, building muscle and reducing stress. What is often overlooked is the fact that we are energetic beings.

A human body is energy and is full of energy. There is a flow of energy experienced much like how blood flows, or the rhythm of breathing. There is also a flow of energy in our body referred to as life force energy, also known in Traditional Chinese Medicine (TCM) as Chi or Qi. This life force energy connects you with every other soul on an energetic and spiritual level.

If you are sitting down all day, then your energy isn't flowing as fully; your body needs to move. You can move in any way that works for you. It could be doing jumping jacks, rotating your ankles, or walking in the neighbourhood. You can take Tai Chi classes, join a rowing team or even just shake; something Moms can do with their kids is shake their sillies out on those cold winter days when the kids just don't want to go outside.

It can be belly dancing, swimming, yoga, running, archery, gardening, or any number of activities. The key is simply to get your body moving in a manner that feels good, is easy to do, and that you love!

We all know what happens when a hose has a kink in it – the water doesn't flow. When there is a kink in a blood vessel, physical symptoms arise in the human body. If there is a pinched nerve, you may lose feeling or mobility in a particular area.

When your Chi is stagnant or blocked, then other health issues develop as well. Trust that your body needs to move at least 45 minutes every day. You need to move your body to do more than just lose weight or because you "should" be doing it; you need to move your body for your life, for your health, and to honour this body you are experiencing life in.

How to incorporate movement into your practice:

Begin your day with some gentle stretches.

Vary your movement routine from day to day - you may go swimming two times a week, do gentle stretching three times a week, and play soccer twice a week.

Add spurts of movement to your regular day, taking a walk at lunch or before an important meeting to clear your head, or walk your children to school.

Mindfulness

Mindfulness is being fully present in the moment. It is the opportunity for you to be present with your thoughts, your words, your body, your surroundings, and your breath. It is being conscious of the "food" you are giving your soul and your energetic field, and the energy you are sharing.

When you are practicing mindfulness, it is much like meditating while experiencing everyday life. It is the action of being aware of your thoughts and letting the ones that are not in alignment with your heart and soul float away. As they float away, you are no longer paying attention to them or feeding them energy.

When you are fully absorbed in the present moment, you easily allow distracting thoughts and emotions to float away and not intrude on your current state of being or doing.

It's been said that the most wonderful gift you can give someone is the gift of your presence. That is true. To be fully present – fully aware of your surroundings and situation – you are also giving to yourself by fully immersing yourself in the current experience.

For example, imagine enjoying a meal with a friend. You listen and fully engage in the conversation with them. You listen to their words, you pay attention to how they speak, and you observe your friend's body language to get a deeper sense of the message she is communicating. You're not thinking about what you want to say next. When the meal is brought to the table, you appreciate the beautiful presentation of the food on the plate and delight in the delicious aromas, eager to enjoy the meal. As you eat, you savour each bite, enjoying how the flavours blend together and how the textures change each time you chew. It is a truly sensual experience.

Being present is truly about activating all of your senses in the current moment to enhance the experience for yourself and others. You are blending all of your senses, and connecting with your heart, mind, body and soul, creating a fully embodied experience.

Your presence also engages those around you. A person who is connected with their soul is consciously present and can uplift any situation.

It may not be possible for you to be present all the time; however, it does get easier as you practice being present in your life more and more.

How to incorporate mindfulness into your practice:

Turn off outside distractions when you are preparing meals: turn off the computer, the TV, your cell phone - just focus on preparing the meal.

When you are with someone, pay full attention to them: their words, their body language, their mood, their energy level. Tune out distractions.

Eat your food slowly and savour the flavours, aromas and textures. Enjoy every aspect of each bite.

Step into nature and observe your surroundings with all of your senses.

Writing/ Journaling

Writing is an expression of your heart, your mind and even your ego. Writing allows an opportunity for you to release some of the energy you have inside of you, rather than keeping it blocked up. As you take time to write down and witness your emotions, you are allowing them to flow, and setting those emotions free. Whether it's in a journal, poetry, a letter, a blog post, or even a story, writing is a way of expressing your inner voice.

Writing allows you to see where you are and to reflect on where you've been. Writing is a valuable tool on your journey and a good place to begin creating a regular practice. You may find that as your soul finds other ways of expressing itself, that you step away from journaling or writing, which is wonderful – you will find that you shift in and out of different practices throughout your journey.

Some people are blocked around writing because they don't like the way they write. They don't like the words they choose or the way their writing looks when they put pen to paper. They may not like that they cannot spell well. It doesn't matter; as the exercise of journaling is for you, you are the only one who has to see it. You will not be judged or criticized; it is like a photograph, capturing a moment in time.

The insights you can gain from journaling are incredible. It is a beautiful journey of self-discovery, capturing "aha moments" as you allow your inner wisdom to come through.

How to incorporate writing into your practice:

Get a notebook, journal or even some lined paper and a binder, and begin to write.

If you don't enjoy writing, but are feeling drawn to try it, start with writing three things you are grateful for that day (a person, place or thing), every night.

Many insights come when you write first thing in the morning when you are not quite fully awake. If you can write in the early morning, be ready for some magic.

Breathing

We reviewed earlier how the breath is a form of energy. Your breath is a very powerful tool that is often underestimated for how it can shift energy. Let us guide you through a very simple example of how powerful a breath is.

Think of a candle. A breath can take a candle from light to dark. It can extinguish it in just a moment. A breath can blow on a dandelion that has gone to seed. You can blow on the seeds, causing that pure potential that is contained in each of those seeds to be set free. A breath on the skin of another whom you love is pure bliss and divinity. A breath is so much more than what keeps you alive. It is life.

To be a breath of life for humankind is what you are here to do and offer. You are life. When you can take the time to breathe in right down into your belly, you are breathing life into your soul. You are breathing life into your pure essence. You are stoking the fire within. Your breath is a powerful tool to shift energy. It can be the difference between stress and peace. It can be the difference between life and death. It can be the difference between wishes unleashed and holding them inside.

Let's move through five breathing exercises right now.

1. Stoking the Fire within Breath - Sitting:

When you breathe quickly, you are energizing your body. In this exercise, sit comfortably, with your back straight and your feet firmly on the ground. Put your hands over your tummy; the left one on your stomach, and the right one on top of your left hand. Breathe in through the nose for the count of five, then exhale forcefully. Do that five more times.

2.   *Stoking the Fire within Breath - Standing:*

Now we're going to do the same exercise standing up. Place your feet hip-width apart and keep your knees slightly bent. You're in a power stance. Breathe the same way: in through the nose for the count of five, and exhale forcefully for the count of seven. Do this a total of seven times.

Notice how you feel in each exercise – the first breathing exercise was done sitting down, and the second one standing up in a power stance. Did you feel more powerful in the second experience? Did you feel more relaxed in the first experience? Reflect on how each of these breathing exercises feels to you. Take a break before you try the others.

3.   *Peace and Quiet Breath:*

When you breathe more slowly, you relax your body. Inhale with left nostril, placing your index finger on your right nostril. Do a gentle breath in for the count of five. Then blow out through your mouth, slowly and gently. Do that three more times, for a total of four.

Be aware of how you feel in that experience. It is a much gentler, softer, and kinder breathing exercise. This is the perfect breathing exercise for you to do before you begin doing a peaceful meditation. It is also ideal when you are preparing to do something very loving, like snuggling with your child or going for a walk in nature. It is the perfect way to ground you gently and instantly.

This breathing exercise is very powerful when you do it barefoot, touching the earth.

4.   *Rejuvenating Breath:*

This is similar to the breath-work that women are encouraged to do when delivering a baby. You inhale and exhale very quickly for seven breaths making the sound "he, he, he, he, he, he, he" and then switch to the haw sound, again inhaling and exhaling very quickly "haw, haw, haw, haw, haw, haw, haw." The haw sound is much like breathing to fog up the window.

When you do the "he" breath, your tongue is raised, When you do the haw breath, your tongue is pushed down. You do not need to think about this, you naturally move your tongue into this position when you make the "he" and "haw" sounds.

This powerful breathing exercise will quickly rejuvenate you in any moment. If you are exhausted and you need revitalization, this would be the perfect breath to energize you.

5. *Relaxing Sleep Breath:*

This breath focuses on an extra-long exhalation. This helps you to let go of the last few worries at the end of the day so you easily and gently drift off to sleep.

You breathe in through the nose for the count of seven and exhale for the count of nine. Do this very gently, counting for the in breath and out breath. If you need to shorten the length of the inhale and exhale, you can. Establish a rhythm to help you settle into a good night's sleep.

How to incorporate breathing exercises into your daily practice:

You can do breathing exercises on your way to work to begin your day feeling calm and peaceful.

You can do deep breathing between tasks to keep you grounded and centered.

You can take a few breaths before you prepare dinner.

You can do the breathing exercises with your partner or children as part of your nighttime routine.

Chanting/Affirmations

Chanting is a sacred technique practiced for over 5,000 years. It is defined as the continuous recitation of mantras, or a phrase or phrases. Mantra is a Sanskrit word meaning, in rough translation, "to deliver the mind." A mantra refers specifically to sacred words and syllables chanted in rituals. You can chant anything. The sounds can have a specific meaning or no meaning at all.

The vibration of the sounds chanted has an impact on humans and is healing to the mind, body and soul. Chants can be repeated aloud or in your mind. Although chants repeated in the mind do not make sounds, they still carry vibration in the universe and within your body, mind and soul.

Affirmations are statements that you declare are true for you. It could be as simple as "I am loving," or "I am joyful." It is a phrase or series of words that you want to be present with. Affirmations are recited, chanted or read repeatedly.

You can recite affirmations that someone else has created or you can choose your own. I recommend that when you recite your affirmations that you complete the set of affirmations with the phrase "I believe." My personal belief is that adding the phrase "I believe" at the end of your affirmations is like sealing what you have said with a full embodiment of trust that it is true, thus bringing those energies forth more powerfully.

Chants and affirmations can be used to uplift yourself when you are in a particular situation where your energy level or vibration is not where you want to be. For instance, if something has happened to make you angry or sad, you can use chants or affirmations to bring you back to a state where you feel better.

Chanting and affirmations are like programming your energy field to a higher vibration. When you chant or repeat a word or phrase, you are becoming present to the energetic vibration of the word or words.

Chanting throughout the day is a good way to affirm your dedication to a particular way of being. "Om" is a well-known Sanskrit chant meaning *the beginning and the end.* It is also used in longer chants at the beginning and/or end.

Singing is even more powerful than chanting, as it raises the vibration of the words and engages different parts of your body and soul. Consider singing the chants and affirmations to which you are drawn. Create any sort of melody that feels and sounds good to you!

How to incorporate chanting or affirmations into your practice:

You can say your chants every time you wash your hands. Write them on the bathroom mirror as a reminder.

You can recite your chant repeatedly as you meditate.

Create your own affirmation and chant them silently as you brush your teeth.

Sample Chants:

Om

Ahum Bharasmi (translates to: I am the universe)

So Hum (this phrase has no meaning)

Sample Affirmations:

I am beautiful, healthy and strong.

I am ready to embrace abundance in all areas of my life.

I am magical.

Nature

Being in nature is like bathing your soul in the essence of the divine. It's a reminder of the beauty that we all are. It is healing, stress relieving, nurturing and revitalizing.

In Japan, *shinrin yoku,* or **forest bathing,** is a common holistic practice. The Forest Agency of Japan first introduced the concept of a "forest bathing trip" to promote a healthy lifestyle in 1982.[1]

Several Japanese studies by researchers at Kyoto University, the Japanese Ministry of Agriculture, Forest and Fisheries and Ministry of Health, Labour and Welfare have revealed many benefits of spending time in nature including: stress reduction, reducing anxiety, depression, anger, fatigue and feelings of emotional confusion.[2]

The power of nature is to be embraced and used for our full benefit. We are one with nature and surrounding ourselves with nature reminds us of that connection.

You can walk in a forest, dig in your garden, sit by the sea, or even look at a picture of a beautiful landscape. In each instance, you are calling forth the calming energy of nature to reset your body and

---

[1] Livini, Ephrat. "The Japanese practice of 'forest bathing' is scientifically proven to improve your health." Quartz (2016) 12 October 2016 (https://qz.com/804022/health-benefits-japanese-forest-bathing/)

[2] Strutner, Suzy. "Why You Need To Try 'Forest Bathing,' Japan's Stress-Zapping Pastime." Huffington Post (2017) 30 July 2017 (https://www.huffingtonpost.com.au/2017/07/30/why-you-need-to-try-forest-bathing-japans-stress-zapping-pas_a_23056175/)

mind, and mirror the beauty within you and every person on the planet.

How to incorporate nature into your practice:

Get a plant - love it and talk to it as you water it.

Plant a garden in your yard and lovingly tend to it.

Visit a local park, watch the magic of nature around you.

Discover nearby trails and waterfalls.

Have a calendar with beautiful nature scenes in your kitchen and create a habit of drawing a happy face on the calendar each day as a reminder to look at the beautiful picture.

Get your camera out and take pictures of plants and animals that surround you.

Expressing Gratitude and Appreciation

The most beautiful way to be in tune with your heart is to be in a place of gratitude and appreciation. Openly sharing your thanks and appreciation for others is a beautiful gift for yourself and others.

It strengthens your heart and soul connection, and your personal energetic signal in the universe.

Every time you thank someone or express how much you appreciate them, you are uplifting their soul, supporting them in being their True Self. You are also setting the example of how to share such a beautiful and simple gift with others.

How to incorporate gratitude and appreciation into your practice:

Create a gratitude journal. Write in it every morning or evening.

Start your morning at work with sending an email to someone to acknowledge something they have done, or to thank them for who they are.

Blessing

My perception of a blessing is you sharing your God essence with another soul – whether it is a person, place or thing. When you bless someone, you uplift their soul and your soul, and facilitate the raising of their vibration, bringing it to a level of its highest potential.

It is common practice to bless a meal, bless a home, or to bless a person when they leave your home at the end of a visit. Experiences at places of worship are often full of blessings.

The more blessings you offer in the world, the more you uplift your soul and those that surround you.

How to incorporate blessing into your practice:

Bless your meal before you eat. At meals, I say:

Thank you to the animals that gave their life. Thank you to the farmers and many hands that brought their meal to our table. And to Mother Earth for helping everything taste delicious.

Bless the driver in front of you (especially if they cut you off!).

Imagine a blessing radiating out from your heart as you hug someone.

Prayer

A prayer is often perceived as making a request of God or whatever higher spirit you believe in. From my perspective, I believe it is more like a conversation where you ask for help, and in turn listen for the response.

I believe that prayer includes:

The act of praying or making the request.

Listening and watching for a response or guidance.

Being open to receiving that response.

Expressing appreciation for the loving support and response.

Prayer is a two-sided conversation. Looking at and recognizing the full feedback loop provides a deeper sense of awareness of the divine connection, rather than a prayer simply being a request.

Praying is a beautiful practice that many people are already familiar with. If this is something you are currently doing, I encourage you to continue.

How to incorporate prayer into your practice:

You can begin or end your day with a prayer.

You can pray whenever you need guidance on how to handle a situation.

Other Possibilties

There are many other activities that you could add to your practice like painting, drawing, composing music, playing the guitar, and singing. I've shared just a handful for you to consider. The key is to discover activities that make you feel good, then consciously do them every day. You deserve to feel good.

Soul Joy

Review your current practice and examine how you can enhance it, whether by increasing the frequency, lengthening it, or adding new activities.

If you do not currently have a practice, look at the examples provided and pick one new soulful activity to add into your day for the next three weeks. Once you've mastered one activity, and have fully incorporated it into your daily routine, add another activity, and you are on your way. Research any activities that make you curious or excited.

Visit my YouTube Channel to find some wonderful meditations to add to your practice:
http://www.youtube.com/user/YourSoulConnection

_____

_____

_____

_____

_____

_____

_____

_____

_____

Chapter 6: Connecting to Your True Self - Your Soul

Making the connection between your soul and your body is the basis of living an incredible and magnificent life. Your soul is your direct hotline to the divine. It gives you access to all you need to know to lead the most magical life possible.

What tends to happen is when something challenging or stressful happens – or you get busy – you forget about this wonderful connection that is available to you. This sidetracks you off your true path, taking you onto a route that provides wonderful learning experiences, but it does not connect you with the most beautiful potential for you.

When you are able to make the connection to your soul, tune in to this connection, foster it, and listen to it on an ongoing basis, your life becomes fun, easy, and playful.

Play is not just for kids and dogs. The truth is that we are so caught up in the busy-ness of life, and take things so seriously, that we forget about how *good* it feels to play. Think of how you feel when you are playing your favourite game or connecting with others in a game. There is this positive energy that uplifts you, energizes you, makes your heart smile, and delight in the time and space that you've given yourself when you just hang loose and have fun.

Play is such a great stress reliever, mood enhancer, endorphin creator. Endorphins are our body's natural "feel good" chemical, so no wonder we feel so good when we make time for play.

Playing is just one of the many ways to nurture your connection to the True You. It's about connecting your soul with your heart and mind; tuning in to that little voice inside – that inner knowing that many refer to as instinct – to get the guidance you are looking for. That is where the magic begins. That is where you get the answers that lead you down the easiest and most rewarding path possible.

You may be asking how can you tune in to that energy.

I created the My Energy Check™ system as an easy-to-implement tool where you can begin to tune in to your energy Physically, Emotionally, Mentally and Spiritually. It's really easy to do. In this system, not only do you learn how to recognize your energy levels, but you also understand how to shift your energy if you are low. You can use energy boosters like activities in your daily practice. Visit jlyall.com/energy to learn more.

You see, tuning in to energy is something we each do innately, but sometimes we forget to pay attention to it. In the section on movement, we talked about Qi, or life force energy. The way most people are aware of this energy is through how they feel, or they can sense how another person, place or thing feels. Consider a time where you may have walked into a room where there has been a heated argument. You can feel the tense energy in that room. By contrast, if you walk into a meditation room or a church, you may feel peace and tranquility.

As you use the My Energy Check System, you begin to understand how you are feeling, causing you to pause and take responsibility for yourself. This shifts your focus to be on self-care rather than constantly going and doing. In the process, you enhance your mind-body awareness.

This heightened awareness enables us to more easily notice subtleties and signals in our bodies, and inspiration that comes to mind. I'm inviting you to begin to do this consciously; pay attention to or "listen" to these feelings more, just like people who "go with their gut feelings" when they make a decision. That is your soul talking to you. With practice, you begin to be able to distinguish the difference between your gut instinct and the ego chatter in your mind. Creating a practice helps you to discern which the voice of the soul is.

Consider this: what if there are no wrong choices in life?

I know that this may seem crazy but what if every choice we make is simply selecting an experience to have- that's it. Some experiences may be more pleasant than others. You grow and learn from each choice in different ways. So often we spend a ton of time agonizing over making a decision, fearful for the outcome. And yet, if we can step back and consider that we are simply making a choice in this situation, and that all we *can* do is make the best selection based on the information we have and how the options make us feel. That's it.

Any energy spent in distress is not serving us, especially since anything that you are meant to do or experience can show up in a million different ways. Moreover, just because something doesn't show up for you now doesn't mean that it won't appear in your life in a bigger and better way 10 years from now.

If you have a dream of being a singer, that possibility could occur when you are a teenager, or as an adult. It could happen in your life through you being a music teacher, a rock star, or singing in a choir. There are so many possibilities of how your dream can materialize; play with the universe instead of being afraid of it never happening.

Every experience is an opportunity for you to go deeper in connecting to the True You and listen to the voice deep inside. The more you practice, the easier it gets; the easier it becomes for you to walk through life's challenges. The more you do to connect to *you*, the more in tune to the messages you will become.

There are a variety of ways you can connect with your soul. One, method is through the beautiful gift I have been given called Connect to U™. The intention of that work is essentially to connect the soul with the heart and mind, and invite the ego to take a break. This soul-stirring program includes a sacred ceremony for clearing Karma, and a Divinely guided meditation that specifically instructs your connection to your soul. Part of the process includes tuning in to your soul to identify the best practices to implement that help you move forward powerfully. It is a simple and delightful experience that can help you accomplish your personal soul connection in very short time.

I offer Connect to U™ as part of my Spiritual Mentorship Program and Intuitive Business Mentorship Program, where I facilitate Connect to U™ in a one-on-one session with me. Or, you can choose to experience the Connect to U™ Self Discovery Program and take the time to tune in to that knowledge for yourself; both options are equally powerful.

I felt immediate, tangible, physical and energetic effects from the energy clearing. Jennifer's Connect to U™ program came to me at exactly the right time in my life. I left confidently connected to my life's purpose and committed to a path and action plan.

Ramona, Toronto, Canada

Other methods of connecting with your soul vary in different cultures, religions, spiritual belief systems or modalities. Some require you to engage in certain practices or training for a period of time (weeks, months, years or a lifetime even) to uplift and enlighten the soul.

You have many different possibilities to consider; the Connect to U™ process that I share is just one. Fundamentally, it is important to choose an approach that resonates with your heart.

Now, connecting with your soul is more than simply having one experience and turning it on. It is about keeping that light on and nurturing your connection. Like the Taoist belief mentioned in Chapter 5, you need to keep putting oil in your lamp.

In the same manner, there are things that you can do to nurture your soul connection, as we reviewed in earlier. These activities include meditation, mindfulness, movement, writing, chanting, breathing, being in nature, blessings, prayer and creating.

In doing these practices, you heighten the awareness of the connection to your soul, keeping you in tune. For instance, ideas and inspirations pop into your head so easily that when you think of things that you need help with, a solution soon follows. The solution can come in the form of a call from a friend, a song, or even a headline in a newspaper. In addition, when you are connected to your soul, you are more open and receptive, so when the answer comes, you instinctively know it is in response to your inquiry. You get that gut feeling – that inner knowing – confirming that it's the answer you were looking for.

Connecting with the True You helps you discover who you are and to be open and receptive to the messages of the universe, causing your life to be phenomenally magical and graceful.

How Connecting with Your Soul Expands Your Love Life

It is quite magical to witness how a "love life" (meaning a romantic relationship – or any of our external relationships, for that matter) is mirrored by what we could call our "Heart Health" or our emotional health; how deepened and awakened the connection between the heart and soul is.

You see, we are vibrational beings, and our soul is our true, divine self. Living our lives according to teachings gets into our head and ego a lot. Moving out of the mind and into the heart strengthens the

58

connection and communication between our heart and soul. It's as if the heart is a better interpreter, so to speak, of the messages from the soul and the universe. When our emotional health (that heart and soul connection) is strong, vibrant, and in tune – just like a happily married couple that is so in love and in tune with one another – we do a better job of sending and receiving messages from our soul and the universe.

Your heart is the most powerful radiator within your physical body. The brain emits powerful thought waves, and yet when these thoughts are translated into their emotional equivalent in the heart, the waves that radiate out are more powerful. In fact, according to the Institute for Heart Math:

The heart's magnetic field, which is the strongest rhythmic field produced by the human body, not only envelops every cell of the body, but also extends out in all directions into the space around us. The heart's magnetic field can be measured several feet away from the body by sensitive magnetometers. Research conducted at HMI suggests the heart's field is an important carrier of information.[3]

As you deepen your connection with your heart and your soul, you will notice little changes in your relationships. The beautiful thing that shifts is that your *love* extends to everything. It's not just a romantic or familial love life or a platonic (friendly in nature) love life, but it truly and indiscriminately expands to every single soul; every single person, place and thing.

---

[3] McCraty, Rollin Science of the Heart Volume 2. Boulder Creek: HeartMath Institute, 2015. p 36 (eBook available online: https://store.heartmath.org/e-Books/soh-vol-two.html)

Therefore, as your emotional health expands, your love life expands. As your love life expands, the magic of what you are creating, touching, impacting and imparting on the world grows, exponentially.

You are like a magnificent radio station. Your heart and mind act like the transmitters projecting your signal. They are broadcasting your ideas, thoughts, and emotions into the universe. The more you are perfectly, easily and readily aligned to the True You, the more your heart and soul are aligned; then you are able to uplift more and more people.

You are able to transform relationships where you previously had witnessed distress. You are able to see these people change because you are seeing them for the love that they are, rather than the problems they were creating in your life.

Anything that shows up for you as a problem is just an example of an area for you to work on:

letting go

accepting

healing

Let's say, for example, that you are good with computers and are an Information Technology (IT) support person. You do a great job helping people one-on-one. Your supervisor sees your potential and invites you to make a presentation to management to help them understand the most common IT problems the company is having and make recommendations for how to work through them. When you make your presentation, you're nervous and you spill a glass of water on your notes. You stumble on your words and forget to share some key findings, and there are times when a colleague just shakes his head at what he's witnessing.

You can beat yourself up for what just happened or you can find opportunities to speak more so you can build your confidence and improve your speaking skills. The presentation gave you the opportunity to have the experience of speaking in front of a group. What happened in the presentation gave you a chance to see what you could change for next time. The experience happened so you could let go, accept what happened as being an experience, choose another experience for next time, and help you grow.

Our acceptance is our true gift to others. Because when we accept ourselves and others for who they are – perfect for who they choose to be at that moment – we are releasing them from the judgments of the past. It is those past judgments that are weighing them down. When we accept them for who they are right now, we are setting them free. We are fostering that individual's connection to their True Self. We are providing the space and setting the stage for that individual to awaken to their gifts. That is the most beautiful gift we can give to another person.

Our full, heart-centered presence uplifts others to shine.

When we can communicate what our goals are, what our dreams are, what our desires are, we are setting the stage for what is possible for someone else. When we can express what we intend to achieve in the world and start to take action steps and make progress, we set the stage for that possibility for someone else too.

When you are able to give them your presence, you are, in effect, extending the hand out to help lead them forward. Help them take that leap of faith so that they can lead a life that they love.

Living life as the True You is about coming in to that place of bliss where you love what you are doing; you are so happy with what you are doing that you look around yourself and you see beauty, pure potential, and possibility. In addition, when you hold that space for others, whether they are conscious of you holding that space or not

- because you are grounded, connected and love - you are opening up a world of possibility for them. When you can truly shine your light and shine it brightly, that is how you illuminate the path for them.

If you are those "few steps ahead" and others who are looking to you for guidance and inspiration can see your light, you are able to show them the way. That is what you are here to do.

You are here to light the way for others to step into their True Self and awaken to their gifts. That is all we're all here to do, to light the way for others. Your gift may show up as an inspiring collections agent who helps people find a way to pay their debt, or a software developer who creates a new time saving tool.

By being the True You, as a parent, as a person, as an employee, as an employer, as a brother, as a sister, as a human being – you are doing great service for this world.

You are doing your duty, because you are living out your life's purpose. You are finding out who you really are. That is pure potential. I love you.

Soul Joy

Take on something new to nurture your connection to your soul.

Pay attention to how you feel in different situations. Begin to notice different ways you receive guidance.

If you are drawn to experience Connect to U^{TM} at this time, then visit jlyall.com

_____

_____

_____

_____

_____

_____

_____

_____

_____

_____

_____

_____

_____

_____

_____

_____

_____

_____

_____

Chapter 7: How Your Soul
Speaks to You

As you start to explore this inner connection, your awareness expands and you begin to notice more synchronicities. It's fun, but can also feel a little strange. You may even begin to think that you are going crazy, as you can try to read into things too much, or you can also find the coincidences that keep showing up to be a little incredible.

You start observing the many synchronicities that are happening, and noticing:

- *Patterns of numbers 111, 444, on the clock, receipts, license plates*
- *Words in the songs on the radio that seem to be answering a question you were just pondering.*
- *Signs – like literal billboard signs along the road – that match what you were just thinking.*
- *So many cool ideas and inspirations that just come to you. For me, a great example is when I'm cooking; I'll get inspired to be creative by blending in interesting flavours.*

These signs can come in so many different ways.

One of my friends, Robin, had an incredible experience when her mother was ill several years ago. While her mother in the hospital, Robin was taking care of her mother's house and her animals. One afternoon, it had been a gloomy and rainy day, and her emotions matched the weather.

As she was finishing up in her house, she was talking aloud to God, and began asking questions. "What should I do? How can I deal with all this?"

When she went outside the rain had stopped and there was a beautiful full rainbow right above the condominium complex. The funny thing about that rainbow is that as she drove away, the rainbow seemed to always stay in front of her, even when she changed direction.

She was stopped at a traffic light, with the beautiful rainbow ahead of her, and she asked God what does this mean? What do you want me to know?

As she was sitting at the traffic light she noticed a large blinking sign ahead. It said in bright letters "change your career."

As she drove past the sign, the rainbow began to fade, and she continued on her way home.

At first she was excited to have received such a clear message. Then the self-doubt began to come in. She kept thinking that she must have misread the sign.

The next day she went to her mother's house again and she purposefully took the same route so that she could check the sign. It said something crazy like "haircuts $10".

At that moment, she was sure that the previous message was sent by the Divine just for her.

Here's another story about how signs show up – one that happened for me. Back in 2010, I decided I wanted to carve out some sacred space for myself, so I created an altar at the end of my dresser. I cleared out a TV and a bunch of stuff, and the last 2 feet of my dresser became this sacred space. The day I did it, a red tail hawk looked at me through my bedroom window. I had never seen a hawk in that tree before. He looked straight at me, as if to acknowledge approval.

You may be wondering: how can you recognize these signs? How do you know it's a sign?

One thing that can help you recognize the signs is to understand the different ways your intuition speaks to you.

You're familiar with your five senses: taste, smell, touch, sight, hear.

We all have the capacity to access those senses at an energetic level – heightened intuitively – plus an additional sixth sense.

Clairgustance	Tasting intuitively - tasting something when you haven't eaten something
Clairaliance	Smelling intuitively- smelling something that no one else smells
Clairaudience	Hearing intuitively- hearing a voice that guides you
Clairvoyance	Seeing intuitively - like seeing an aura, a vision
Clairsentience	Feeling an emotion or getting a physical sensation in the body - like "truth bumps"
Claircognizance	Your sixth sense, your gut feeling, your inner knowing about things

Your soul and the universe speaks to you through all of your senses, and we each tend to have one or two intuitive senses that are more dominant. I have a few friends whose dominant intuitive sense is Clairvoyance, and they see people's auras as they walk around. That's just how they see people – with soft colours around their body.

My dominant intuitive senses are Claircognizance and Clairsentience, and the other ones show up too. I'll get a vision which may simply be an object, or like a 3 second video clip on the movie screen in my mind's eye. When I cook, I get different tastes to blend together. And occasionally I'll smell mint when no one else can, or my uncle's favourite tobacco that he used to smoke in his pipe.

To help you with recognizing the signs, I recommend meditation. It's a fantastic tool to help you to quiet your mind and turn down the volume on the inner chatter so you can listen to the voice of your soul more easily. When you're able to get quiet in meditation, you begin to appreciate little gems of quiet moments outside of meditation too. These are the moments when your soul can easily speak to you through your intuitive senses.

As your awareness expands, you begin to get into a rhythm of recognizing these signs as the answers to questions you have. And as this recognition begins to feel natural, you effortlessly progress to understanding what the signs means.

Understanding the language of your soul

Seeing the signs is one step; however, understanding what the signs mean are another thing. The tricky part with this is understanding what the signs mean relevant to you, your life and your future. Just as two people can watch a movie and each get something different out of a movie, you can observe a sign, and it can mean one thing to you and something completely different to someone else. Both observations can be correct for each individual.

I have people asking me for help with understanding what the signs they see mean. I can share insights to consider, but I prefer to empower them with how to discover the answers for themselves.

As we are getting started with this translation and deciphering, we need to look to outside resources as a beginning point for understanding possible meanings. Even as you refer to these resources, you still need to understand what is true for you – or relevant to your life – as you decipher those messages.

Here's an example:

I had a yellow finch pecking at my window the summer of 2012. It happened several times and I thought it was strange, but ignored it. Then finally it happened again when I was in a session with a client. The client said that her grandmother told her that when a bird pecks at a window, that it meant that someone was going to die.

That didn't feel right for me, so I looked up what the animal totem of a yellow finch means and the essence of the message was:

Finches are a sparkly omen of high energy and bright days on the horizon. Native People of North America see the finch as a bird of happiness.[4]

And this felt right to me, with what was happening in my life at the time.

That's the key: when you decode these messages, go with the answer or translation that feels right.

Those translations and messages can come from so many places- books, articles, another person, or just an inner knowing.

Here's another example:

I was at a networking event, where I met a lovely woman named Vicki. She is radiant and fit, with long golden brown hair. She's a Massage Therapist, and at the time was studying to become a Holistic Nutritionist. She told me she was deciding what to name her company, and she liked the word Nourish, but wasn't sure. As

---

[4]Venefica, Aviva. (n.d.) *Bird Meaning Finch.* Whats-your-sign.com. https://www.whats-your-sign.com/bird-meaning-finch.html

soon as she said it, I could feel it was a fantastic match for her energy. I told her how important that word was for her and her business; both as a Massage Therapist and for what she was stepping into. She was surprised by this. She left our conversation a little uncertain with my feedback, and also curious.

That weekend she went to a health care practitioner marketing workshop where they focused their energy on developing their brand and marketing plan. As she contemplated her branding language and overall brand, she came to realize that the feeling of the word Nourish was indeed important to her - she came to recognize what that feeling inside of her was, and our conversation helped her to understand that. It indeed felt right to her too.

The more you practice observing and begin to expand your awareness, letting go of control for how things need to be, the better you get at understanding your soul's language.

Here's another example:

At a wellness event in 2010, I met an incredible Native Canadian teacher who was making a presentation about earth-based spirituality. Her skin was tanned, and she had long black hair with a thick, contrasting, white streak of wisdom through it that hung down next to her face. Her all-knowing eyes spoke just as loudly as her voice. As soon as I heard her speak and felt her words, her energy, her presence, I knew she was my teacher. And I told her so, right after her presentation.

I took several workshops with her and loved her broad knowledge over many cultures and how her teachings blended them. However, over time I saw a firmness in her that didn't really resonate with me. But I knew she was to be my teacher, so I investigated her longer programs to go deeper into her teachings.

She has this incredible four-year Priestess program, and my soul was so drawn to it, and yet also felt so impatient because this program was so long. I craved something just as deep, but faster. Her assistant told me that they get that comment a lot, and the program was simply the way it was. They said it was up to me, if it felt like a good fit, then go for it.

Then some of her teachings didn't resonate with me, didn't resonate with how I wanted to move forward in life. It made me feel uncomfortable. And yet, I was "told" by the universe that she was my teacher. So I explored her program further, and after she provided more information, she said, "and now, I leave it up to you."

Something didn't feel right inside, so I left and I never went back to another one of her workshops.

I was mad and frustrated for a few days. My gut had told me that she was my teacher and now I felt horrible - what's up with that!!!?

One morning a few days later, I was replaying the experience in my head as I was getting dressed, and I pulled out a pair of black socks to wear. I was about to put them on when I realized that it was not a pair of socks. It was a close match, but not a perfect match. The patterns on the socks were different.

That was the message.

She was my teacher, for that time, but our student-teacher relationship was complete for that part of my journey.

I had an awareness to know what those two different socks meant. It was exactly the same colour, but a different pattern.

It was close, but not quite a match.

And again, I FELT the answer in my heart and soul. That's what stopped me in my tracks: the knowing. Here's the distinction I want you to recognize: I went from that little tantrum in my head of needing to know what was going on, to dropping into my heart, to recognizing the feeling of KNOWING the answer in my heart.

(Note: This teacher is absolutely incredible. I have so much respect for her and her workshops, and programs are amazing, comprehensive; the workshops taught me so much about spirituality. This experience was simply my intuition telling me that my time with her was complete. It was shortly after that, that I channeled my modality, Connect to U.)

Rather than finding the answer that satisfied my brain, it was about finding the answer that felt right in my heart.

This simply takes practice.

It's a combination of observing, and an awareness of what is going on in that moment of observation – noticing the feelings, the sights, the sounds, the tastes, the sensations you're having – and then trusting the interpretation that comes to your heart and soul. That's one of the biggest steps in this process: trusting that what you perceive is true.

What you're doing is interpreting different forms of energy. The language of your soul is in the form of energy. People naturally interpret energy all of the time. We put together those impressions to determine what it means.

Sometimes the meaning doesn't even make logical sense. However, you just know that it's the right thing to do, or the right answer. You develop a trust in the feeling and interpretation. You build this trust with practice, just like how you would build your confidence with any language. You need to start using your intuition every single day.

Soul Joy

Discover what your dominant intuitive sense by joining the Intuition Game, 7 days of games to help you connect with your intuitive senses. You'll receive a meditation to help you understand what your dominant intuitive sense is:

jlyall.com/intuitiongame

Start to write down some of the synchronistic events you witness in your journal. See what patterns you notice.

If you find that there is something in particular that is "speaking to you" like numbers, symbols or animals, learn more about it. Research it online, borrow a book from the library, find a workshop or course.

_____

_____

_____

_____

_____

_____

_____

_____

_____

_____

_____

_____

_____

_____

_____

_____

_____

_____

_____

CHAPTER 8: BRINGING IT ALL TOGETHER

While our conversations have been quite light-hearted and easy to work through, I want to discuss what tends to be the biggest stumbling block for people: *how do I live a soulful life in a world that seems so out of tune with its own soul?*

The planet we live on is the perfect place for you to begin the journey of connecting with your soul. The variety and contrasts around the world help to bring clarity to the experiences you have had, and act as a barometer for your progress.

You can see this as you witness your reactions to situations that would normally generate a particular response in you. When you notice that you react differently – perhaps sailing through calm and cool, diffusing any problems before they are able to escalate – that's your signal you are living from your soul. Bingo! Progress has been made!

You simply need to be you, and continue to evolve. There is no need to worry about how someone will react to who/how you are now. I can guarantee you that your ability to live from your soul will positively affect others, consciously and unconsciously. You will be a role model for them to consider as they work through their personal soul's journey.

You see, situations come up in life as an invitation to go inside and do some inner work. It may show up as unexpectedly losing your job, a death of a loved one, always feeling out of place in life, an accident, or a health issue.

I remember the first few months that I was just starting to learn about my soul. I was at a point in my life when I didn't feel like I was doing what I was meant to do. I felt like something was missing in my life. I felt like I had a calling to do more and be bigger than who I was at that moment. Yet, I had no idea how to figure out what to do to understand what direction to go in.

I became drawn to spiritual experiences. I had an intuitive session called an Akashic Record Reading. I discovered crystals and dowsing. I took courses to learn about the medicine wheel and the Celtic calendar.

My perception of the world was changing. I felt different. I remember dreading family and social gatherings because I felt like I had changed so much that I had no idea what to talk to other people about anymore. I was concerned that they were going to think that I was weird and judge me for the way I talked.

I threw out my back in the strangest way. I was simply leaning on my bed (my feet on the floor). I was bent forward, reading a book, my elbows resting on my comforter. And when I went to stand up, my back just didn't feel right. Then it started to feel stiff and uncomfortable to move.

The only way I could get through the day was by meditating and doing yoga in the morning before everyone else woke up. I had to take care, as sitting or standing for long periods hurt. I dreaded going to bed, because I was in so much pain whenever I tried to turn on my side or get out of bed.

I went to several family gatherings and survived. No one thought I was weird, although I did feel stifled because I was afraid to express myself fully.

I had created a big ball of stress in my gut that spread through my whole mid-section, including my lower back. I remember I had a dream that I went to the washroom and my intestines came out. Somehow, from that, I deduced that my stomach was in knots and I needed to unravel it.

The next night just before bed, I asked my husband to stand over me and imagine that he was pulling a rope out of my stomach, hand over hand. I asked him to keep going until I told him to stop or he felt like he was done. Once he was done, 85% of my pain was gone. I woke up the next morning and was able to get out of bed. By the end of my morning routine of yoga and meditation, I was perfectly back to normal. I had released that stress and worry and could function properly again.

You see, what happens in our lives has to do with what is going on in our heads and our heart. If we are in a state of worry about how we're going to fit in, we will put ourselves in a state of dis-ease. If we simply focus on honouring ourselves, and being kind and loving (which are all good things to be, right?), then we can walk through life with grace and ease.

The bottom line is that you simply need to tune in to your heart and soul and do your best to speak, think and act from this place. To tune in, simply create a daily practice where you invest time in self-care, getting quiet and paying attention to how your body feels; giving yourself a break from the busy-ness of the day is all that it takes. The My Energy Check™ System is the perfect tool to build your mind-body-soul awareness. You start to be aware of your thoughts, your intuition and the sensations in your physical body more and more in your everyday life.

Make the time for your practice in your life, otherwise you won't find the time. The more you do, the more you will enjoy your life and the happier people around you will be.

That's it. Be joyful and happy as we are meant to be~

Easier said than done, you may think. Actually, it is truly a state of mind over matter. If you use the tools outlined in Chapter 5, you will find it easy to achieve.

The truth is that we often judge ourselves more harshly than anyone else does. When you are extending love into the world, remember that love extends to you too. Being kind, compassionate and loving to yourself will make it easier for you to be this way with others. Take care to honour and love yourself first, to give you the confidence to share yourself freely without fear or inhibition.

A miracle is waiting to happen and it starts inside of you!

Soul Joy

Review your current practice. See if there is anything different that your body needs today. Your practice will change and grow as you do.

Ask yourself "how much do I love myself on a scale of 1 to 10?" Then write down the messages that come into your heart regarding the rating you gave yourself. Ask for ideas for how you can shift the rating higher, or to keep it high.

Visit jlyall.com/energy to learn more about My Energy Check^{TM}

_____

_____

_____

CHAPTER 9: REMEMBERING WHO YOU ARE

As we travel on this journey, the intention is to take you back to who you really are; to remember your true potential when you live a life full of love, not fear. When you are able to live from this place, you are able to fulfill all that your soul chose to do in this lifetime.

Your soul is an incredible being that has all intelligence. The only stumbling block is remembering or learning how to "crack the code" and access it. Cracking the code is actually quite simple; it happens when you remain calm, clear and centered, and are not caught up in other people's dogma, stories, or lives.

Our greatest limitation is actually the fear that others impose on us. The good news is that as you stand stronger in the Truth of who you are, the easier it is to recognize games the ego is playing with you and others.

Removing the boundaries to success lies at the place where you stand in your Truth. Standing in your Truth is like standing in an open field with endless and luscious green pastures spread out in front of you, with no obstacles in sight.

You can re-create yourself in every moment (it's never too late). You can re-establish your connection to the True You in a heartbeat. When circumstances arise where you are momentarily bombarded with information or emotionally overloaded, you have tools – like meditation and affirmations – to keep you centered and grounded in the knowing of who you are.

You are this boundless potential that can accomplish anything you set your heart on. Use your heart as your personal Global Positioning

System (GPS) to help guide you closer to the resources and steps that you need to take to accomplish your dreams and goals. Let your heart simply draw you to - and draw to you - all that you need.

Your job in your physical body is to begin the momentum of the energy flowing through taking action. Just like a set of dominos all lined up, it takes the action of gently pushing the first domino for the beautifully planned out pattern to flourish and the chain reaction of events to take place.

Remembering who you are is one of the most important steps of this whole process. This is why the inner work is important. It is your soul support system. It keeps your heart and soul connected with your mind. When your mind gets distracted or caught up in things, your tools – like deep breathing and chanting – help you stay in tune with your soul, so as not to be swayed by others who have not yet made that connection.

Standing in your Truth is believing in yourself with unwavering strength and knowing that what you see as possible is true. Your dream can indeed be accomplished, with firm belief. It is your success and beliefs that help inspire others to believe in themselves and their possibility too. As more and more people are focusing energy on that possibility, it brings the dream forward more quickly and more powerfully, gaining momentum like a tidal wave of love and joy.

Believing in yourself is not something to just consider doing *sometimes*. It's not something that you say you're going to do, and then forget about. To truly step into who you are, you need to believe in yourself and your true potential with your whole heart.

The past is irrelevant and the future is yours to create. You do not need to know how to accomplish your goal; you simply need to have the tenacity to find the resources and the courage to move forward with your idea, despite what others say.

Believing in who you are remains your greatest asset. There are no insurmountable tasks. Everything simply takes patience, practice, trust, action and most of all, belief that it is possible. There are a million ways that a goal can be reached, so if something different happens than you expected, persevere and try another approach.

Many great inventors tried different designs and formulas for their creations. While working on a method to create a commercially viable light bulb, Thomas Edison allegedly said, "I have not failed 1,000 times. I have successfully discovered 1,000 ways to NOT make a light bulb."

You can apply the same dedication to making your dreams come true. It takes the strength and ability to know who you are to help you have the courage to see it through.

One test that remains is for you to remember your Truth without feeling the need to meet the standards of others. Other people – who are not in touch with their soul – are unable to understand the drive, courage and stamina that is pushing you forward with such grand desire. And eventually, as I found, these people will fall away from your life.

That test, the resistance of others, can feel like running into a brick wall at times, but it too will crumble with your firm belief.

Remembering who you are resembles a dream state of existence, different from that which others perceive. It is the seeing of potential and possibility – in not only yourself, but in others – to be able to uplift them to a place where they can also fuel the dream for you and themselves, giving the dream more energy to flourish.

It's time for you to remember who you are and build your dreams.

Soul Joy

Take time to reflect on who you really are, letting go of labels from the past or what your current career or social circumstances may be.

What is your Truth? What ideas, causes and topics stir something so deep inside of you that you feel compelled to do something about it?

_____

_____

_____

_____

_____

_____

_____

_____

_____

_____

_____

_____

Chapter 10: Is it Really that Simple?

It's hard to believe that this guide is coming to a close. Although you may think that a soul is more complicated than this, and that there is more to learn, the truth is - it really is quite simple. When you embrace these concepts, you allow yourself to tap into the most magical resource to lead you through life: your soul and soul support system.

It's not complicated. People make it complicated with their stories, their analogies, and perceptions, but it's really quite simple. The first step is to surrender and then let yourself be guided to what feels right. For me, I wasn't happy with the way my business was going, so I gave myself permission to take time to tune in to what I really wanted to do. It was that little intention that started the ball rolling for me. It led me to have an Akashic Record reading that opened my heart up to a new possibility I had not even thought of.

Consider the fact that we all know how to be healthy: eat well, exercise and keep life balanced. Yet there are so many stressed-out and overweight people in this world. We know what to do; the question is whether or not we act on it. The same is true for connecting to your soul. Can you be courageous enough – brave enough – to not let your True Self falter? When you begin to take the steps to nurture your soul, you will notice shifts in your life.

For instance, when you are connected to your soul – the True You – and you encounter a difficult situation and you realize that you don't react to it the same way that you used to. Instead of yelling at someone or complaining about someone when you witness something that is out of alignment with who you are, you let go of that anger and frustration by taking a deep breath. In that deep breath, you recognize they are just like you: a soul on a journey and thus you respond in a gentler way. That's how you know that you have embraced these concepts. That is how you know that you are in greater control of your life than you'll give yourself credit for. That is when you'll know that you are surrendering to the divine flow and connecting with your soul.

As we go through life, we experience waves of self-doubt, worry and uncertainty. Consider *A Beginner's Guide to the Soul* as a resource to keep you on track with who you really are. We are all destined for greatness; the question is simply whether or not we are willing to walk that path. Finding the courage to connect with your soul and step into your true potential is the greatest gift you can give yourself and every life that you touch.

So when you have those moments when you wonder:

Do I really matter?

Can I really make a difference?

The answer is always: *absolutely yes*. Believe it is possible. Carve out your vision and you shall achieve it. The possibility of it all happening begins in your heart and soul. The success of it happening depends on your belief in that possibility.

The road to believing in your potential and the most awesome possibility available to you includes:

Giving yourself the space to tune in to Who am I.

Understanding what a soul is.

Accepting who God (or the higher power you believe in) is in your life.

Welcoming love into your life.

Nurturing your soul by investing in delicious self-care every day.

Connecting with your soul: opening and developing the communication channels between your soul, your heart, and your mind.

Bringing all of the above together in your daily life.

Remembering who you are.

Embracing the simplicity of living life from the soul.

You see life is meant to be playful, joyful and happy. It will be sprinkled with moments of sadness and frustration and anger, that is human nature. The contrasts of life help you to appreciate the joyful moments that surround you. When you are able to live from your divine nature more than your human nature, then you know that you have mastered the art of connecting with your soul.

EPILOGUE

Wow! I first began to channel this book in 2012. I finished writing the first draft it in 2013. And I sat on it. I waited. I had so many excuses of why I couldn't publish it: I couldn't afford it, it was too hard, too complicated, I had other priorities. I couldn't decide if I should just do a pdf, or ebook, or publish a book; perhaps I shouldn't publish the book, because it is no longer a reflection of who I am, so it's now out of context…and so many more excuses.

And yet, I've always known that this creation wanted to be seen. Wanted to be read. I knew that somewhere, there was someone who needed to hear the ideas and concepts I share.

I would take a small action step, and then put it the book aside, focusing on other projects. And it sat here waiting, patiently.

It took me 8 years to publish this book. To finally honour it and let it be seen.

What was the catalyst?

The universe nudged me to create a program called **Ready To Be Seen**: to clear away blocks, beliefs, and energy that are standing in the way of you stepping into your power in your business, and taking courageous action to be seen in the world. To be in integrity, I felt I needed to publish this book.

So truly, neither I nor the book needed to wait that long, and yet I trust that the timing that this book has landed in your hands is perfect.

I share this because if there is something burning in your soul that you truly want to do, that is a little scary, or out of your comfort zone, I'm encouraging you to go for it. It won't be nearly as big as the story you are creating in your head. Any challenges or hiccups along the way will simply be growth opportunities for you. You can do it!

I believe in you.

About the Author

Jennifer Lyall mentors ambitious female entrepreneurs who feel stalled in their business but don't know why - or how - to get through their current ceiling.

Women who have this inner knowing that they are being called into something bigger, but lack the clarity on what to do or where to put their focus?

Incredible souls who want to deepen their inner connection and use their intuition to confidently move forward in their business.

She supports them in learning to master their energy and intuition so they can uplevel their impact and income, while doing what makes their heart sing.

Jennifer is known for...

Million dollar decisions. She has helped million dollar entrepreneurs make some of the most important decisions of their life using the best decision making tool available - their gut instinct. Using her signature program she helps connect the wisdom of your three minds (logical, emotional and intuitive) so that you never doubt your inner guidance again.

Tuning into you. She helps ambitious women get clear, focused and productive in a way that makes their heart sing. Her genius is tuning in to the energy of ideas, people, places and situations to help you prioritize in your business and create a plan for moving forward.

Inner Battery Check. Energy is everything. As a long time energy worker and intuitive, not only does she read your energy, but she teaches you how to master yours giving you more confidence and stronger boundaries. You start to live your life as the True You.

You can learn more about Jennifer, Connect to U^{TM} and how to transform your energy by checking your Inner Battery at: jlyall.com

Connect with Jennifer:

Linked In: https://www.linkedin.com/in/jlyall/

Facebook: https://www.facebook.com/LivHealthybyJL

Instagram: https://www.instagram.com/livhealthybyjenniferlyall/

Manufactured by Amazon.ca
Bolton, ON